GOOD COOK. FRIENDLY. CLEAN.

BROOKE ROBINSON

CURRENCY PRESS
SYDNEY

GRIFFIN THEATRE COMPANY

CURRENT THEATRE SERIES

First published in 2018
by Currency Press Pty Ltd,
PO Box 2287, Strawberry Hills, NSW, 2012, Australia
enquiries@currency.com.au
www.currency.com.au

in association with Griffin Theatre Company in 2018

Typeset by Currency Press.
Printed by Fineline Print + Copy Services, St Peters, NSW.
Cover design by Re.
Cover photography by Brett Boardman. Cover image shows Tara Morice.

A catalogue record for this book is available from the National Library of Australia

Contents

Good Cook. Friendly. Clean was first performed by Griffin Theatre Company at the Stables, Darlinghurst, on 4 May 2018, with the following cast:

B	Fayssal Bazzi
SANDRA	Tara Morice
A	Kelly Paterniti

Director, Marion Potts
Designer, Melanie Liertz
Lighting designer, Alexander Berlage
Sound designer and composer, Nate Edmondson
Stage manager, Khym Scott

CHARACTERS

SANDRA, female, 58, wears a hat or scarf to cover her hair
A, female
B, male

A and B are different characters in each scene, never older than 35 years of age.
A change in scene also indicates a change in house / unit location.

A NOTE ON THE SCRIPT

A slash (/) indicates the next line of speech begins at that point.

This play went to press before the end of rehearsals and may differ from the play as performed.

SCENE ONE

A *and* B *are onstage.*

B: I'm glad you're home
A: *We're* glad
B: She'll realise
A: You're home!
B: It's too much
A: Pleased that you are home right now
B: We never say that
A: Hi Sandra
B: Keep it simple
A: Hiya Sandra
B: Hey housemate!
A: Buddy!
B: Mate
A: Hello!
B: How was your day?
A: That's good
B: This is awful
A: Do we have to do this?
B: Can't we write a note? Stick it on the fridge
A: 'Hey Sandra! By the way … '
B: House bye-bye
A: You. House. Bye-bye
B: I could draw it
A: Symbols. Softer than words
B: A couple of stick figures. House with two rectangular windows, chimney and squiggly smoke curling out
A: We're outrageous
B: Send her a text
A: Throw a few emojis in there to round things off
B: I'm not looking forward to this
A: Can I get you a biscuit?
B: That's nice

A: How about a biscuit, Sandra?
B: Distract and placate with food
A: Spiky sugar rush before we give you the bad news
B: I'll have some mugs out, as if I was about to make tea the minute she gets in
A: She likes tea
B: She does like tea
A: And we're nice
B: We notice
A: We're thoughtful like that
B: Then we'll say …
A: We were just about to have a hot drink
B: There's this study that proves if you hand someone a hot rather than cold drink in a business or a date scenario
A: A date scenario?!/
B: They're more likely to feel receptive toward you
A: It's literal
B: The warm or cold feeling in their hand moves to their heart, exactly/
A: I was at the supermarket earlier and
B: She called and asked me to check your cupboard to see if you had any Tim-Tams?
A: Back me up, if I freestyle, won't you
B: We know they're your favourites
A: I may go off-script, heat of the moment
B: They are, aren't they?
A: I think so
B: Sandra's favourites
A: They definitely are
B: I said you looked to be out
A: So I picked up a packet
B: Would you like me to open them, Sandra?
A: How about a nice cup of tea?
B: We're leaning too much on the tea
A: Would you like that, Sandra?
B: She would. She'll take it. She'll like it
A: We wanted to catch up tonight
B: Straight away

A: To give you plenty of time, Sandra
B: The minute this came up
A: We've barely talked about it ourselves, have we?
B: No
A: No
B: We should both say 'no' at the same time
A: No
B: No
A: Have we?
B: *This* is us discussing it
A: We're thinking it through as we speak
B: As long as you know we haven't been …
A: Plotting?
B: Well …
A: Scheming?
B: I was going to say *planning*
A: Much better
B: We wanted to … immediately, with you
A: Chat. And see …
B: Be completely upfront
A: We wouldn't do this
B: If it wasn't for a really good friend
A: You know him
B: Sandra hasn't met him
A: She has an idea, we've discussed him
B: We must have
A: He's come up in conversation
B: He has a lot to think about
A: He's nervous about the job
B: It's a significant promotion
A: New responsibility, he works in charity
B: The pressure, you can imagine
A: Not-for-profits, in this climate
B: He's a saint
A: Saint's a bit much
B: I've seen him buy cage eggs in Coles
A: That doesn't surprise me

B: He doesn't have any family. We're his closest friends in Sydney
A: We'd offer the couch
B: He could crash in the living room
A: On the carpet
B: By the rug
A: He'd be happy on the floor
B: Curled up under the coffee table with a pillow
A: He's that kind of person
B: Except, well
A: We don't have a living room
B: It's one of the major disadvantages of the property
A: That's good
B: 'Disadvantages of the property'
A: No living room …

SANDRA *enters, unseen. She carries two shopping bags.*

B: What else?
A: We don't have time to brainstorm
B: Let's go over it again
A: Once more
B: I hate this
A: She's lovely
B: She's really quite lovely
SANDRA: [*joking*] Talking about me again?

A *drains to white.*

B: No
A: No/
B: No!
SANDRA: Are you saying I'm not 'lovely'?
A: 'Course you are
B: That is not in dispute
SANDRA: I've decided I want to be one of those people who buys themselves a snack for the bus ride home from the supermarket. But not someone who gives in to temptation and cracks open a packet of something that was on their shopping list—it has to have been bought specifically for the bus, a reward for/
A: We need you to move out

B: That was abrupt

A: We have a friend moving to Sydney. He's taking, we're giving him the room

A beat.

B: Are you …

A: Could you say something?

A short beat.

B: I hope this hasn't …

A: [*to* B] Not *you*, Sandra

No response yet from SANDRA.

B: I hope this hasn't, I hope *we* haven't

A: Have we said something wrong?

B: We have

A: Haven't we

B: Oh god

A: We have

SANDRA: What sort of time are/

A: Not tomorrow or

B: Anything/

A: Crazy like

B: No

SANDRA: A couple of months, we're talking about months …

B: Well

A: I think it's open

B: Flexible at this stage

A: As flexible as we can be when something

B: *Unplanned* happens and

A: But he is, I mean he is

B: Moving in in two weeks

A: So it is

B: There is an urgency

A: To the 'situation', can I call it that?

B: I think you can

A short beat.

A: So is this okay?

SANDRA: This is a joke
A: Should we talk timeframes?
SANDRA: You're playing with me
B: How about two weeks?
SANDRA: Let's finish off that curry I made. Are you hungry?
A: [*to* B] That would work
SANDRA: I have pappadums …
B: Yes I think so
A: We're saying two weeks
SANDRA: It's spicy
B: Done
A: That's a relief
SANDRA: Sit, I'll heat it up for you
A: From yesterday?
B: [*to* SANDRA] No don't heat it/
SANDRA: You can't eat it cold/
B: I mean, 'yes' two weeks from yesterday

A brief pause.

SANDRA: I thought we could all sit in the kitchen. I've been dying to tell you about my trip to Aldi this morning
A: It's not that/
SANDRA: As I'm walking in, a guy's caught stealing a huge bunch of bananas/
B: That we/
SANDRA: Listen. Listen/
A: We/
SANDRA: Stuffed down the front of his jeans. Security guard, the one we like, the big one, gets his hand down there and pulls them out, one by one, and/
A: It's not …
SANDRA: That isn't the end of the story
B: We want you to know …
SANDRA: Is there something I …
A: No
B: God no
A: I want to make that clear

B: It's not
A: It's absolutely not
B: *That*
SANDRA: They weren't even the expensive fair trade ones
A: We wouldn't
SANDRA: The bananas

A short beat.

B: You know we wouldn't
A: Obviously the timing isn't
B: Ideal, for you
A: We wish it weren't the case
B: It's definitely not *why* this is happening
A: We're not …
B: Monsters
A: Especially after
B: It's been two years
A: They've flown!
B: Two really nice years
SANDRA: Four
A: Wow
B: [*referring to* A] We were strangers too
A: When we moved in
B: We're doing this for
A: Our friend
B: Long-standing friend
A: We've always wanted to live together, we've been saying that since we met
B: If ever the opportunity arose, haven't we?
A: We would definitely, we would have to take it
B: And then he gets a job …
A: Not just in Sydney
B: But in Surry Hills
A: Would you believe
B: He was headhunted
A: He wasn't even looking
B: You see

A: So we couldn't say
B: No
A: It's the world telling us this is happening whether we like it or not!
SANDRA: It doesn't have to happen/
A: And we don't
B: No
A: Like it
B: He's moving here from Melbourne
A: Doesn't know anyone
B: He comes to us, his new friends
A: And asks if we will take him in and with the rental market …
B: You understand
SANDRA: I don't
B: As long as you know, Sandra …
A: It's not
B: We want you to know, that it's not
A: An excuse or
B: A convenience or something
A: Because …
B: What's most important to us
A: Is that *you* know this is coming from a place that is
B: Genuine
A: And it has nothing to do with/
B: Not at all

A short beat.

SANDRA: [*referring to the curry*] I should heat this up
A: I feel like we should …
B: Have you got a few more minutes, Sandra?
A: This isn't how I imagined
B: No one wants to leave things
A: Hanging

A short beat.

B: I mean obviously we're not *leaving* things *tonight*
A: This conversation
B: That's what I meant
A: How about a drink?

SANDRA: Alcohol?

A: I've cider in the fridge. [*To* B] You've got craft beer

B: I do

SANDRA: I'm okay

B: A sneaky drink

A: So things feel

B: Stitched together

A: Make sure the air is/

B: Clear

SANDRA: I won't

B: I'll pour small glasses

SANDRA: [*firmly*] I can't

A short beat.

A: That was stupid

B: Sorry

A: I forgot because you're looking so well!

B: Really well

A: But the sentiment, we do want to leave this, here tonight and *later,* on good

B: Because it hasn't been all bad has it?

A: Not at all

SANDRA: I thought we … had fun … enjoyed each other's company

B: It's been good

A: Frequently great

B: Really great

A: On second thoughts

B: Yes?

A: If we could make it Monday week

B: [*to* A] What are you thinking?

A: As the move out date?

SANDRA: That would be/

B: That would help us enormously

A: It would give us a chance to fix up the room before he arrives

B: We said we would, didn't we?

A: We did say that wouldn't be a problem

B: That's a relief

A: We really appreciate this, Sandra
SANDRA: You appreciate …
A: You will be getting your bond back
B: In full, of course
A: Because you've not trashed the place
B: Not at all
A: Ha-ha!

A short beat.

B: You've been very clean, actually
A: Notably clean
B: We do want to leave this on good …
A: … You never once clogged the shower with your hair. I mean even, even before …
B: Oh my god
A: When you *had,* it never, I never found clumps of your hair, your brown hair clogging the drain

A short beat.

B: [*to* A] Did you just …
A: God I
B: You're nervous
A: I avoid confrontation, I'm not accustomed to
B: At least you didn't say 'grey'. [*To* SANDRA] You're not grey
A: I didn't. But you did
B: You're not good at this
A: No

B *comforts* A.

A: You know that 'hair clogging drain' is a particular annoyance of mine
B: She does have a hair thing
A: Only when hair is in *drains*, I don't have a generalised 'hair thing'
B: No
A: I think …
B: Woah, look out!
A: I was going to say, I think hair is … overrated
B: Agree

A: I want to say that I appreciate over the years
SANDRA: Four years
A: That you have never once clogged the drain with your, when you had hair

A short beat.

A: It's often a problem, isn't it? In sharehouses a number of people using the same bathroom. The bath or sink starts to drain slower and slower and you know soon it's going to come to a complete stop, and you'll be left with a dam, a still pool of filth and water and hair and someone's going to have to put their hand in there and clear it. Our shower is temperamental. Thin pipes or …
SANDRA: I'm going to go and/
B: [*to* A] Why is that?
A: About the drain?
B: Do you have a theory?
A: I mean maybe, Sandra, your hair is sparse or soft or just good hair
B: Great hair
A: And that's why
B: It never clogged the drain
A: Why it fell out so quickly after you begun …
B: That explains it
A: It's going to grow back fabulously
B: Of course it will
A: You hear, people say that after it will grow back *better,* you'll love it, you'll be so *pleased*
B: That's why some people shave their heads don't they? Even if they don't necessarily have to
A: My hair's fried, years under the straighteners …
B: Your hair's great
A: Hair dryers on full whack. Maybe it's something I should do. What do you think?
B: I don't know
A: Sandra. Do you think I should?
SANDRA: I don't think that's necessary
A: It's not just hair, really, it's more of a … a whole bodily thing. I don't like coming into contact with someone else's/

B: Dandruff?

A: I can't stand other people's fevery sweat or vomit or blood …

B: Nobody *likes* blood

A: Or the air when they cough or being in the same room as a sneeze or their skin peels or they have a sore and I can see it or a bit of bandage poking out from underneath their/

B: Mother Theresa over here …

A: I can't help it

SANDRA: A mouthful of this Chicken Madras and you'll change your mind

B: You'll find somewhere else

SANDRA: You couldn't possibly give up my curries

A: You will

SANDRA: Who's having mango chutney?

A: I know you will

SANDRA: Extra chilli. Red. Seeds and all

B: You'll settle in and you'll like your new place better

SANDRA: How you like it

A: Wish you'd moved years ago!

SANDRA: Are you going to eat? You're waiting for me to try it first?

No response from A *or* B.

I'm the guinea pig. It smells hot. I'm first. It can't be that hot. It can. You're just going to stand there and watch me? Okay. It's just me. Okay, I'm going in. I can do this. Argh! No. I don't know if I

SCENE TWO

A: Are you the hairdresser?

SANDRA: I've been known to trim a few ends

B: Belinda, one o'clock interview?

SANDRA: Sandra. One fifteen

B: Sandra! Welcome. You're early

SANDRA: Some days, just occasionally, your bus and train connections work out beautifully

A: Someone said they were a hairdresser

SANDRA: I'm not trained. I can manage a bowl cut if that's what you're after
A: My fringe is starting to stab me in the eye
B: That person went straight to the shortlist
SANDRA: You even have your scissors out
B: I told her that didn't look casual
A: I'm desperate for a free haircut from a stranger
B: She almost put down a sheet
SANDRA: So there's two bedrooms in total?
B: We need someone to take over the agreement for at least six months
A: Your side of the agreement
B: You'd be replacing me in the flat
SANDRA: I'm looking for somewhere long-term
A: Not that the concept of 'agreement' carries much weight around here
B: How are you placed, Sandra?
SANDRA: I'm ready to move next week
A: Don't feel locked in, will you, that's what he's trying to say
SANDRA: But it's no great rush
A: He didn't. Feel locked in
B: I'm buying an apartment
A: I'm staying. He's moving out
B: That's the animosity you may be detecting
SANDRA: Good for you
A: I'm the last of my friends *not* to buy
B: It must be about to crash. The property market
SANDRA: It does seem imminent
A: They've been saying that for years
B: What have I done?!
A: He was promoted last month. Now earns twice as much as me
SANDRA: Big mortgage?
B: Catastrophic
A: I bet Sandra's bought somewhere, is that what you're doing, renting it out until it's all paid off?
SANDRA: No I've been renting for/
A: Never?
SANDRA: I've never had a mortgage
B: See

A: How long would you be wanting to stay?

SANDRA: Indefinitely

B: We know this isn't anyone's idea of the rest of their life

A: This is a stop-gap for you for a few months while you save for a deposit

SANDRA: I'm not saving for anything in particular

A: We signed a two year lease together

B: Private landlord, did we mention, lives in the main house

A: We'd suck it up in a granny flat while each of us saved for our own place

B: Repairs are fixed very promptly

A: By then we'd hate each other, so we'd flip a coin, one of us would get the Eastern suburbs, the other would get the Inner West and never the two shall meet

B: I saved a little faster than anticipated

A: He met someone

B: That didn't have much of an impact

A: An investment banker

B: I'm still contributing

A: He's paying the stamp duty. That's it

SANDRA: It doesn't mean you own it, not really, does it, it's the bank

A: He's on the ladder, it'll increase in value and they'll sell up and I'll still be/

SANDRA: If the ladder were real/

A: I'm getting left behind, I am behind, and I've been left. [*To* B] You're ditching me

B: I'm not leaving you

SANDRA: Not everybody buys

A: I know that

B: Some people rent forever

A: That's what I'm afraid of

B: She's waiting for her father to die so she can inherit his apartment

SANDRA: Is he ill?

B: When he's over for dinner it's stuffed crust pizza. Garlic bread. Everything deep fried

A: If you have any ideas about how I can get him to eat cronuts for breakfast I'd really like to hear them

B: The side effects of taking cholesterol medication repeatedly dropped into conversation

A: He's seventy-one and still runs the half marathon

SANDRA: You don't need your father's money

A: Oh I do

SANDRA: You don't have a house but you also don't have debt

B: That's right

SANDRA: You don't owe anyone anything, you're free to/

B: Listen to Sandra

A: I'm going to be out by July. We're only asking for a six month commitment.

SANDRA: Six months with the possibility of extension?

B: I'd say a strong possibility

A: Oh God

SANDRA: Don't worry, if I moved in, I could stay until you drop me at the old people's home

A brief pause.

Free bowl of mushy peas on arrival

B *laughs much more than the joke deserves.* A *doesn't.*

B: You Sandra, are funny

A: It's not a party house

B: Noise travels across the backyard, but they're quiet too

SANDRA: I'm in bed by eleven

A: I assume you're not into parties

SANDRA: Not at all

B: We don't mean to assume because/

SANDRA: I'm not

B: We share a weekly organic vegie box

SANDRA: I'd be very interested in a vegie box

B: Which I'll cancel after the free trial period

A: Do you have much stuff?

SANDRA: I don't

A: No bicycle?

SANDRA: I'm more of a walker

A: There's no storage space. Or parking.

B: She's thinking of taking up cycling

A: No I'm not

B: No you're not. I said that because I thought it sounded normal and you still need to recover from the hairdresser thing

SANDRA: You seem very normal

B: She's great to live with

A: I take the bins out. That's pretty much as good as I get

SANDRA: I recycle

B: Sorry?

SANDRA: Green waste. Compost. I only buy recycled paper

B: Oh, the eco stuff, don't worry about that, love

A: [*to* B] You put it in the ad

B: You have to, don't you, every sharehouse ad says they're eco-friendly

A: But we're really not

SANDRA: I don't mind either way

B: I love chemicals. Anything toxic. CFCs. Sniffing aerosols got me through high school

A: Why haven't I seen your new place?

B: We've only just exchanged contracts

A: You've been around there a few times, you could have invited me along

B: It isn't mine yet, we won't have the keys until next month

A: Why haven't I see any pictures?

B: What's to see, at the moment it's someone else's house, you don't want to look at a random's ugly sofa

A: You must have photos

B: Not really, I/

A: Are you afraid I won't like it?

B: You'll love the kitchen, and the bathroom, I know you're mad for a double sink

A: You haven't even shown me the floor plan from the real estate agent

B: Why would you want to see that, it's boring/

A: You don't want me to see that it has two bedrooms

A very brief pause.

B: It's a study, a/

A: I knew it!

B: For storage. Basically a walk-in cupboard

SANDRA: I've lived in one of those
A: You don't want me to move in with you
B: It's not that, I/
A: I'm fine to live with in a shithole but you don't want me messing up your shiny designer flat
B: I've adjusted to your cleaning standards, I love your mess, I want you around, first weekend, okay, I want you there to make everything look … lived-in
A: I'm going to starve here
B: You won't starve
A: The organic vegie box will stop coming and I'll be eating dog food
SANDRA: I'm a good cook
B: Ask nicely and Sandra might give you some lessons
A: Tinned dog food
SANDRA: I'll start you off with toast
B: You probably won't have to eat pet food of any kind
A: I'll have to marry Ralph in Accounts. He's paying off a unit in Penrith
SANDRA: Nice high ceilings
B: The windows are double-glazed
A: So it costs twice as much if you break one/
SANDRA: I bet it's cool in summer
B: Warm in winter/
SANDRA: In winter!
A: What if dad leaves his apartment to that woman he met on Tinder. I think I'm hyperventilating
B: Take it easy
SANDRA: The little patio's great
B: North facing
SANDRA: Morning sun
B: Perfect spot for plants
SANDRA: Some herbs
A: I'm going to ask him. Outright. Tomorrow
SANDRA: Ralph?
A: *Dad*
B: [*to* A] I'll get you some tea
SANDRA: Plus there's a laundry in the garage, is that/

B: Included and free to use, you don't get that everywhere
A: I've gotta get out of here
B: [*to* A] Breathe … the camomile's coming … [*To* SANDRA] Sip of that and she'll be fine
SANDRA: You have a very decent place
A: You're just being nice
B: No she's not. [*To* SANDRA] But you are very nice
SANDRA: I mean it
B: When are you aiming to move in, Sandra?
SANDRA: Two weeks
B: But you said you could also do next week
SANDRA: If that suits you
B: It suits her perfectly
SANDRA: Easy
B: We'll speak to the landlord. We're seeing one other person
A: The hairdresser
B: We'll call you
SANDRA: Excellent
B: We will

SCENE THREE

B *is engrossed in a video game.*

A: What I can say about this place is we have solid walls. In my last house, my room was next to the toilet. Walls as thin as a meth head. Someone goes to the loo in the middle of the night and it would sound as if they were peeing straight into my head, direct from bladder to brain. Five of us living there, once you count partners sleeping over, there could be ten people in the house, all getting up to wee at two, at three, at four AM. One of the housemates was an actress. Always on a juice cleanse, chugging green fluids all day, she'd need the toilet every hour, the constant noise, it dripped into my subconscious and I started dreaming about other people's wee flooding the world. My flat white turns out to be urine, my miso soup: urine. It was the first thing I heard in the mornings and the last thing I heard at night. The endless rush and slosh of liquid all around me, the bed tilts, eyes closed, I want to get back to sleep, I'd try to imagine I was sleeping on a cruise ship, that I'm being carried away on a wave in a very small very expensive room with a perfectly round cute little window and a casino down the hall, and I'd try to relax, float above it, enjoy it and maybe I could if it were an actual cruise and clear blue water instead of PISS! I tried to get all the housemates to basically stop drinking altogether. I found this disease, you know there's an illness where your body tells you that you're insatiably thirsty, it can't turn off the signal and you drink and drink until you drown internally. I told everyone in the house that my aunt died of this internal drowning disease and I didn't want any of them to die from it too so they should cut down, they should only drink one glass of something a day and I'd police it, for their own good. It worked for a while but they'd sneak glasses of water when I wasn't around, and they'd be up again in the middle of the night waking me with their streams of piss.

I'd have this recurring dream where I'd go to the red cross on George Street to donate blood and it's thin yellow urine instead of plasma that leaks out of my arm and I'm mortified but the nurse's face is the most frightening thing, she's not surprised at all, like I'd discovered this secret that she already knew, I guess she was told at nursing school, that human beings are seventy per cent piss, cut them open on the arm, the toe, they nick themselves shaving and that's what comes out, that blood is like, a mirage, or a cultural construction and something which the medical establishment, Coca-Cola, Medicare, the UN and definitely international governments were all in on. But. Here we have solid walls so you can feel free to drink your diuretic of choice well into the night and wee as frequently and as late as required without hesitation

B *looks up at* SANDRA *from his video game. He shoots her and she explodes into pixels.*

SCENE FOUR

SANDRA: I've lived in a warehouse with seven others. No hot water. A six-bedroom terrace with nine people and one bathroom. Above a twenty-four hour kebab shop. A blow-up bed above a squat above a pub. An Edwardian place which still had the toilet in the backyard. Someone had attempted DIY to connect it to the back of the house but they obviously gave up half way so one side of the extension was just a tarpaulin. The jars were never clean so we'd drink from recycled ring-pull cans, the rims are a little sharp until you get used to it

B: We're looking for someone

SANDRA: Laidback

A: Easy-going

B: Energetic

SANDRA: That's me

A: We've all just graduated. I did commerce

SANDRA: [*to* B] And you?

B: Engineering

A: The vacant bedroom

SANDRA: Yes

A: It's …

B: Illegal

A: Technically

SANDRA: There's no window. It's a box room

A: It's to do with the size

SANDRA: I. Personally. *Like* a box

A: It's supposed to be a spare

SANDRA: I like squares, preferable to living in a triangle …

B: We've a $45,000 HECS debt

SANDRA: I've a track-record in successfully challenging water and electricity bills

B: We can't afford to keep an empty box

A: You've lived in a triangle?

SANDRA: A square, a rectangle, a semi-circle, and a room where the walls were uneven and the ceiling started to cave in, I think that counts as a trapeze

B: We have mice

SANDRA: Mould?

A: Proper black fur. Give it a pat and it purrs

SANDRA: I come highly skilled in killing spiders

A: The light on the stairs hasn't worked for months

B: How's your eyesight?

SANDRA: When you walk up the stairs in my current place, you have to hold the handrail for support, because otherwise *it* falls over!

A: The light in our kitchen flickers when you turn it on and you'll probably feel a buzz travel up your arm

SANDRA: Fun

A: We keep an old wooden spoon hanging from the doorknob on a piece of string. If you're tired of getting shocked you can use that to turn the light on and off

SANDRA: There's your engineering degree in practice!

B: The area's dodgy

SANDRA: Lidcombe TAFE karate class 1998, 'most improved'

A: Before we moved here …

B: I lived in Lavender Bay

SANDRA: With your family?

A: On a homeshare

B: Run by the local Council

A: They place someone young in the home of an elderly person who lives alone

B: I did it for a year

A: One hundred a week for a room on the harbour

SANDRA: I haven't paid a hundred dollars since the nineties …

B: Antique furniture, oversized living room, Persian rugs, books, piano, conservatory round the back … owned by seventy-five-year-old Anna

A: The low rent is in exchange for ten hours of help around the house each week

SANDRA: Could be fair

B: The contract says you have to stay home five nights a week in case she slips and breaks a hip in one of her marble bathrooms

A: The ten hours of work became twenty

B: Then thirty

A: He did her shopping, cooking, laundry, cleaned the house

B: Poured her glasses of vintage sherry and hoped she wouldn't piss herself on the couch which I'd then have to clean

A: They sold it to him as a program that helps young people beat the housing crisis in return for friendship with an older person

B: It's a way of swinging a free carer so they can stay in their three million dollar houses

SANDRA: Shameless!

A: He became her slave. She had dementia and was losing her inhibitions. She'd touch his leg, unbutton her top

SANDRA: Oh

A: I told him I was cool with it, go for it! Close your eyes!

SANDRA: Argh!

A: She took his watch. Turned up weeks later. In her undies drawer! Then his shoes. His sunglasses, in January. The dementia makes them steal stuff. Anything within swiping distance of her arthritic knuckles. Old people …

B: Steal from your fucking coffin if they could

A beat.

A: Are we … I think we're supposed to ask about your job, your routine

SANDRA: It's only the first thirty seconds that count when we meet someone. You've already made up your mind about me

B: Have we?

SANDRA: You can't help it

A: So

SANDRA: Ask me whatever you like

A: Okay, I …

SANDRA: Ask me if I

B: Do you believe in extraterrestrials?

SANDRA: I have my fingers crossed

B: How about ghosts?

SANDRA: No

B: Autobots or Decepticons?

SANDRA: Decepticons, obviously

A: Are you a morning or a night person?

SANDRA: Night

A: Favourite animal?
SANDRA: Miner Bird
A: Favourite colour?
SANDRA: Off-mustard
A: Well that's the end of the formal applicant vetting process!
SANDRA: Did I pass?
A: You're in the lead
B: Except we're not allowed dogs
SANDRA: I don't have any pets
A: We thought you …
SANDRA: Nope
B: On the rental website
SANDRA: Oh, that's only a dog from Google images …
B: Your profile picture
SANDRA: I like to use an animal stand-in
B: Defeats the purpose though, doesn't it …
A: I never use a photo of myself for those things …
B: … If people don't know who you are
SANDRA: Sorry
B: … Who to expect
SANDRA: I'm not a cute dog
B: Your picture looked more puppy than dog
SANDRA: Woof!

A brief pause.

You two seem fun
A: Do we?
SANDRA: I think we'd get along fine. Have some laughs
A: You're pretty cool
B: Do it
A: Ah?
B: We agree. Do it now
A: [*to* B] Yeah?
B: Sandra, would you like to move in with us?
SANDRA: I would …
A: Yeah!
SANDRA: … Love to!

B: Can you draw a clock for me?
A: [*checking her watch or phone*] It's eleven thirty
B: Draw a clock face. Showing half past six, can you do that?
A: The pub on the corner does life drawing classes on Tuesdays
SANDRA: We should go!
B: Spatula. Forest. Grapefruit. Forage. Lead. Circumspect
SANDRA: ?
B: Repeat the six words
A: What is this?
B: Can you recall them?
SANDRA: Ah … Spatula …
A: We don't own a spatula
B: [*to A*] Shh
SANDRA: … Grapefruit … Forest. Circumspect. Lead. I forgot one

A brief pause.

B: 'Forage'
SANDRA: 'Forage'!
B: One more time. Teapot. Squash. Switch. Toe. Wire. Arrangement
SANDRA: Teapot. Squash. Switch. Toe … Wire … Arrangement
B: I said 'teabag', not teapot
A: You said/
SANDRA: I heard 'teapot'/
B: It was 'teabag'
SANDRA: Oh
B: You guessed
SANDRA: What does that mean?
B: Your memory's failing
A: Let me try
SANDRA: You're testing my memory?

B *turns on the torch function on his phone. He approaches* SANDRA *and holds one of her eyelids back while he inspects her pupil like a physician.* SANDRA *laughs nervously and tries to play along. She sticks her tongue out and makes an 'Ahh' sound, but it doesn't get a laugh from* B.

What are you doing?

B *doesn't respond.* SANDRA *is uncomfortable but goes along with it.* B *moves on to her other eyelid and continues to inspect her pupil.*

What's in there? Do I have a soul?

SANDRA *has stopped laughing and tries to shake* B *off.*

A: What are you doing?!

B *grabs* SANDRA*'s face and kisses her hard on the mouth. She recoils.*

What the fuck!

B: [*to* SANDRA] You heard her. I have a free pass with geriatrics

SANDRA *is humiliated,* B *is restored.* SANDRA *gathers herself to leave.*

A: I'm sorry, Sandra

SCENE FIVE

SANDRA: I hope you don't mind, I signed for a package for you. I arrived as the delivery guy was half way through filling out the card and I hate when I miss a package, it's such a hassle to have to get to the Post Office

A: I always forget my ID and by the time I get to the front of the queue my little boy's turned the place over. Thank you!

SANDRA: Sandra. It's 'Sandra'

A: Sandra! Once I missed a package and whatever I'd ordered was only worth twenty dollars so I never collected it, it was easier to just write it off. What are you doing on Tuesday, could you be here to let the plumber in?

SANDRA: I'm not as good with tradies, delivery professionals are my main area of expertise

A: Excuse the mess

SANDRA: It's a beautiful house

A: I bet your place doesn't look like this

SANDRA: No … no it doesn't

A: I'll make some coffee. Give me one second, I've been on hold with Telstra since eight

An alarm goes off.

SANDRA: Is everything ok?

A: That's only a timer. *William that's your beep beep. No more screen time. Put the iPad down!*

B: *I'm playing!*

A: You've had two hours

B: More!

A: Put it down, William. Put the iPad on the table

B: No!

A: You know the rules. Play with something else for a while

B: Argh!

SANDRA: Can I help with anything?

A: *Jesus Christ not the scissors!*

SANDRA: Maybe I can …

A: *Scissors are not toys, put them down. William. Now!*

SANDRA: Are those your crayons William?

B: My crayons

SANDRA: Did you draw that?

B: Me draw

SANDRA: That's so good, aren't you clever

B: I draw houses!

SANDRA: I can't draw like that. You're very good

B: Lots of houses!

SANDRA: Could you draw something for me?

B: Big houses!

SANDRA: I'll take a big house. That would be lovely

B: A green house. Green and orange. Stripy house

A: Doubt I have a future interior designer on my hands

SANDRA: How old are you William?

B: I'm four

A: I'm so sorry about this. The chaos of working from home. I'm meant to be showing you that we provide a peaceful living environment

SANDRA: That's lovely, thanks William, I'll put it on my fridge. Why don't you draw another one?

A: I suppose you see inside a lot of houses in an average week, I hope we're not the worst

SANDRA: That'd be the one with the shoe propping open the door all day and night because one of the inmates never remembers their keys

A: God! Student housing. I don't know how you stand it

SANDRA: Neither do I!

A: Do you find you can you switch off, can you walk down a street without peering in through every window?

SANDRA: You can't help but transport yourself for a second, imagine what you, what your life would be like if it were on the other side of the door

A: How long have you been doing this?

SANDRA: This time only for a couple of weeks

A: That's why I didn't meet you last year

SANDRA: Your outgoing lodger has been here for a year?

A: We like to keep them turning over every twelve months. Unless we found someone perfect. I have a feeling you can help us with that

SANDRA: I hope so too

A: I know you're going to say the photos aren't up to scratch

SANDRA No, I/

A: My husband took them. Everyone's a photographer these days. Except for him

SANDRA: The ones in the ad?

A: And they've got to be good, don't they, to get the millenials' attention. Instagram filters in the kitchen. Animated GIF of the bathroom

SANDRA: They were good enough for me

A: We deliberately didn't include too many of the house

SANDRA: You want people to come and see the place in person …

A: It's a separate room, you can't very well show off the nice living space and then say sorry lodger, you're not welcome to use it

SANDRA: I didn't expect to

A: We forgot a bloody photo of the bathroom. We'll take one now

SANDRA: I can just look at the bathroom

A: It wasn't the best ad

SANDRA: In all my years I can honestly say I've never made a decision based on a bathroom

A: This'll be our third lodger. All through your university

SANDRA: My old university? Really? Oh yes, I said in my email, and you studied at/

A: We haven't had any problems

SANDRA: That's good. That's/

A: You noticed we raised the rent from last year

SANDRA: Well I guess inflation

A: It's still fair

SANDRA: Two hundred

A: I know Youth Allowance is going down, but ours have been international students anyway …

SANDRA: Right … seems … reasonable

A: It's weird isn't it, not to include a photo of the bathroom

SANDRA: Why don't I help you with the coffee?

A: Won't you have students asking? Is it an ensuite or an out-house or a chamber pot under the bed type situation? You might be bombarded with emails

SANDRA: They all just snapchat these days, I assure you, very few young people can compose a decent email

A: And when you get back to the office, you can decide whether you need it in the ad or not

A brief pause.

SANDRA: Send it to me by the end of today

A: It's good to see the university protecting its students

SANDRA: I do my best

A: The only other thing I failed to mention is we sometimes negotiate reduced rent if our lodgers are willing to commit to some regular babysitting. Now that you've seen William in full flight you may come to the conclusion that not every student will be able to handle him as you did

SANDRA: Well they're only eighteen, nineteen, aren't they?

A: I try and only leave them alone for only a couple of hours until they get used to each other

SANDRA: I'd worry about whether you can trust them. Did you read in the paper that story about all of these millennials texting the emergency services and then wondering why an ambulance hasn't turned up

A: I'm sure our last lodger would have tried to get hold of the police on WhatsApp

SANDRA: It's the moodiness that gets to me, the lack of social skills, empathy

A: Locked away in their room for days on end

SANDRA: Light leaking under the door at all hours

A: I do wonder what the hell they're doing in there

SANDRA: I had a student recently. I was telling him about something I'd seen out the front of the university, police officers forcing a man strip down to his underwear on the street, while they searched him for drugs. I'm relaying this story and the student, he's eighteen, stops me, interrupts me to say I was wrong to start telling him this anecdote without first issuing a trigger warning

A: I'd believe it

SANDRA: A summer's day and they all melt

A: I had one put his dirty clothes in the dishwasher. Couldn't tell the difference between that and the washing machine. Another blew up our microwave by putting her mug of milk in there for thirty minutes and walking away. Her parents had always done everything for her, she had no idea

SANDRA: And they're all lactose intolerant and gluten free and allergic to everything

A: After the microwave incident I put a trail of peanuts in a semicircle around the kitchen, that kept them out

SANDRA: I don't work for the university

A brief pause.

A: You're employed by the agency

SANDRA: I'm looking for a room for myself

A: I don't know what you mean

SANDRA: I saw this listing advertised through the University. I'm here to see the room

A: For...?

SANDRA: For me

A beat.

I can move in immediately

A: You're a student
SANDRA: No
A: A mature student?
SANDRA: I just came across your ad
A: Oh
SANDRA: Should we start again?
B: Mummy: Choccy!
SANDRA: I'm still interested in the room, I/
B: Mummy!/
A: I should have mentioned that the lodging comes with a tiny, screaming neighbour, the spare room is right next door to …
B: Choccy!/
A: I've been wasting your time
SANDRA: I could move in this week, I/
A: [*to* B] You win. One square of choccy. Don't tell Daddy … [*To* SANDRA] Let's hope he remembers these treats in fifty years when he's choosing my nursing home …
SANDRA: I can operate a landline phone, a washing machine and a microwave. No allergies. William would be safe with me
A: I'm not sure you saw the full advertisement
SANDRA: I saw it
A: Not all the details are online
SANDRA: I got the gist
A: It's a single room lodging
SANDRA: Yes
A: You saw that
SANDRA: Two hundred, bills included
A: The room comes with a single bed, a desk, lamp, and a small TV/
SANDRA: Small TV
A: There isn't much storage space
SANDRA: I know there's a bathroom!
A: There is a bathroom. We're both freelancers, my husband and I. We work from home most of the time, so we're looking for someone who's often out of the house. Students suit because they're in class all day, at the library, a night job perhaps …
SANDRA: You wouldn't see much of me
A: William does tear around the house

SANDRA: I wouldn't notice

A: Thank you so much for coming!

SANDRA: Could I see the kitchen?

A: The kitchen?

SANDRA: Do your lodgers usually have access to the kitchen?

A: Of course

SANDRA: You said you both work for yourselves?

B: Gummy bears!

A: [*to* B] Go and wash your hands

SANDRA: I don't have children

A: Oh?

SANDRA: I'm not married

A: I see

SANDRA: I'll do my share of the cooking. How do you split chores with your husband?

A: That's the lodger's cupboard

SANDRA: Wait till you try my lasagne, do you like lasagne, William?

B: Yuck!

SANDRA: I always share the telly remote. Never take up the whole couch. Kick my shoes off at the door. Board games are nice when Netflix gets too much. I'm not bad at Scrabble. I guess we'll watch a lot of ABC Kids! Maybe a bit of *Dancing with the Stars*? I bet William likes that. Are you a good dancer, William?

B: Argh!

A: We let our students use the living room when we're away over summer

SANDRA: I understand this is a family home

A: And you've seen the lodger's bathroom so that's it really, thank you

SANDRA: Do you need to see my references, payslips, or a/

A: That's ok

SANDRA: I like music

A: Thanks again for coming

SANDRA: Outside of work, I go to a lot of concerts. Oasis. Nirvana. The Stone Roses. Silverchair

A: Have a nice evening won't you

SANDRA: That's my era

A: You're talking about our posters in the hall?

SANDRA: No, I/
A: You walked past them coming in/
SANDRA: I mustn't have been paying attention
A: We collect old concert posters
SANDRA: I love this one, Nirvana, 1992, Big Day Out. Bought one that day myself
A: You went?
SANDRA: My memory's hazy, but I was there. Do you get to many concerts these days?
A: Depends on our student babysitter
B: No babysitter!
SANDRA: I've retired from mosh pits

She lifts her hat or scarf.

Decades of punk haircuts and fluorescent dye, my hair couldn't cope, I had to shave it off. I've had my last green Mohawk. It'd be my pleasure to babysit. [*To* B] We'd have fun together wouldn't we, William?

A: I didn't mean/
SANDRA: I'd be very happy with that arrangement
A: I'm sorry about the misunderstanding with the room
SANDRA: Have you had many students express an interest?
A: I need to talk to my husband
SANDRA: Will he be home soon?
A: Not for an hour
SANDRA: It's no trouble to wait
A: I've really got to get William's dinner
SANDRA: I'll help. Give me a job to do
A: It just needs heating up
SANDRA: What's on the menu?
A: Soup
SANDRA: I know a great recipe/
A: Let me speak with my husband and/
SANDRA: I can come back later tonight
A: I don't think that will suit
SANDRA: I could pop by again later in the week
A: We'll keep that in mind

B *becomes increasingly agitated.*

SANDRA: I'll bathe the baby. Change his shitty nappy. Watch cartoons. Have inane conversations with him. Be bored out of my brain. Vacuum, scrub, cook, fold. Wash a forty-five-year-old man's underpants, pick the dirty ones up from the floor, ball his socks, do what you gotta do to have a roof over your head!

B: Hate soup!

SANDRA: I'll wait over here until your husband gets home

A: Look I've really got to get/

B: Yuk!/

B *lets loose a full-scale tantrum. This time* SANDRA *can't tame him.*

SANDRA: It's no bother. I'll wait/

A: That's not necessary/

SANDRA: Pretend I'm not here

B: More choccy!

SANDRA: We'd have fun if I babysat wouldn't we William?

B: More choccy!

A: Dinner first

SANDRA: Wouldn't we William?

B: [*to* A] No!

SANDRA: Don't you want to talk to your Auntie Sandra? Hey? Hey William? You shouldn't be shy around your Auntie Sandra! Hey! Hey! Come on! Don't you want to talk? You don't have to be shy around me. William! William!

A: Goodbye

SANDRA: We can settle this tonight

A: Goodbye Sandra

SCENE SIX

SANDRA *is unconscious.* A *holds two fingers to* SANDRA*'s wrist to check for a pulse.*

B: Let's start today

A: Let's not panic

B: Starting from now
A: Jesus okay
B: Our diet is bad. We have a poor diet. We drink more than the recommended daily limits. We do not exercise
A: We should run, we have ten pairs of joggers between us in the hall
B: We're killing ourselves. Slowly, so we don't even notice we're doing it
A: We're noticing now, we're looking right at it
B: That's the wine subscription cancelled
A: It's not too late
B: And the coffee beans
A: This is our wake-up call
B: Death has come into the house
A: But we'll overpower it
B: We'll change
A: A plan
B: I'm going to smash our wine glasses
A: Start small, with some gradual improvements
B: We start today
A: Oh that's right
B: Clean eating. Raw and unprocessed and clean
A: It'll be okay
B: We can turn things around
A: We can be like those people who live to 110 but refuse birthday cake because of course they don't eat cake because that's how they got to 110 in the first place
B: Exactly
A: Our efforts will pay off
B: We'll be rewarded even more than people who ate well and exercised their whole lives because we were on the wrong track and we worked really hard to turn things around and everybody knows that's worth more than if you were on the right track the whole time
A: We will need some leeway
B: A day off a month
A: A week
B: A day off a week to eat to drink to do whatever we like
A: To prevent backsliding

B: To prevent total rebellion from the regime

A: We'll drink we'll eat chocolate and ice cream and fried chicken and brownies and bricks of solid, solid delicious filth but it's only a day a week so it's fine

B: Exactly

A: The rest of the time we exercise. We eat boxes of fruit. We start tonight. By cleaning out the fridge and the cupboard of anything and everything that is bad and unclean, anything that's going to kill us and make us sick we'll throw it out

B: We could …

A: Get it all out of the house

B: … Instead of throwing it out

A: We could eat it

B: Go berserk

A: One last time

B: Demolish everything in sight

A: Make ourselves sick in a preventative way like the way a vaccine deposits a tiny dose of the virus inside you but it's ultimately to protect you from getting the full-blown thing

B: Tonight we're going to eat junk food to save ourselves

A: I'm not going to die in a bedsit surrounded by cold chips and Aldi bags

B: I won't be found in my studio having choked on Iced Vo-Vos three days earlier

A: We should find Sandra's phone. Where's her bag?

B: In the living room

A: You get it. I'll get the Kit-Kats

A *and* B *exit.* SANDRA *regains consciousness. She doesn't know where she is. The space feels very large and empty. She's alone for a full minute.*

A *and* B *re-enter with* SANDRA*'s handbag.*

You're awake!

SANDRA: Sorry

B: Are you okay?

A: What happened?

SANDRA: Just a little … brain snap

A: You fainted
SANDRA: Snap
B: Do you do that often?
SANDRA: No!
B: Ever before?
SANDRA: Never!
A: Should we call an ambulance?
SANDRA: I was just inspecting your flooring. The carpet thread count is extraordinary
B: Maybe you should go to the hospital?
SANDRA: I'm okay
A: Is there anyone we can call?
SANDRA: I'm fine, really
B: Can we get you a glass of water or … something to eat?
A: Maybe your blood sugar's low?
SANDRA: I just ate
A: You look pale
SANDRA: I'm always pale
B: We … you'd already been out for a minute or two …
A: We checked to see if you had one of those diabetes bracelets on? We looked inside your handbag
SANDRA: Why don't we start again?
A: I hope you don't mind. About your handbag
B: Take a seat for a moment. Lay down if you like
A: Feel free to sprawl
B: There's no need to hurry
A: Stay for as long as you need
SANDRA: Let's get on with the tour. What were we up to, the laundry?
A: The laundry?
SANDRA: You said there was a laundry room?
A: Ah
B: Yes …
SANDRA: I'm ready now
B: You still want to see it?
SANDRA: Yes
A: Oh …
B: Okay …

A: Well …

B: I guess we could

Neither A *nor* B *makes a move to resume the house tour. A short beat.*

SANDRA: Were you expecting me to leave now?

A: No, I/

B: Not until you're ready, you can stay here/

A: Lay on the couch

B: Rest until you're feeling up to it

A: We don't want to push you out

B: Are you sure we can't call someone?

SANDRA: Let's keep going

A: Ah …

A short beat.

SANDRA: How long was I out for?

A: Unconscious?

B: I'd say two

A: Closer to three

B: Probably four minutes

SANDRA: Surely the room hasn't been taken in that short time?

A: No, I

SANDRA: You haven't offered the room to someone else in the past four minutes

B: Of course not

SANDRA: Then what's the problem?

B: We want to make sure you're okay

A: Maybe you'd like to come back tomorrow when you're feeling better?

SANDRA: You're seeing others this afternoon?

A: We have a few interviews scheduled

SANDRA: Then you'll offer it to someone else by tomorrow. I'm here now. Let's keep going. Ask me your next question

B: Well …

A: Ah …

SANDRA: What have you been asking the other potential housemates?

A: Ahh …

B: I can't think of anything else
SANDRA: *Ask me your next question*
A: Well, ah …
B: You'd be able to pay the bond this week?
SANDRA: Of course
A: Rent is three hundred a week
SANDRA: Great
B: And bills come to about four hundred every quarter
SANDRA: Extra, bills are/
B: Say five hundred to be safe
SANDRA: But that's included? You've factored that into the price?
B: It's not/
A: I don't think that's included/
SANDRA: That's not on top of/
B: Actually our wifi plan is going up next month/
SANDRA: Right
B: Did you think/
SANDRA: Got it
B: We weren't clear
A: We made it sound/
SANDRA: You didn't, you/
B: As if the three hundred was inclusive/
SANDRA: My fault/
A: Sorry
SANDRA: No problem at all

SANDRA *wobbles on her feet, her legs give way as if she is about to collapse again.* B *and* A *both react and try to catch her.*

SANDRA *recovers.*

A: Woah!
B: I was going to say we're looking for someone relaxed and laidback but you're really relaxed
A: I'll call an ambulance
SANDRA: Ah ha! That was a test!
B: You should sit down
SANDRA: I was just testing your reaction, to make sure you're not serial killers. Do you know the best way to check if someone's a

sociopath? Yawn. It's contagious. If someone doesn't yawn back, no empathy. You can also faint and see if they catch you

A: Oh!

SANDRA: You passed!

A: We can drive you somewhere, to a medical centre, your GP?

B: A taxi would be quicker

SANDRA: Next question!

A: Ah, so … what … what do you do in your spare time?

SANDRA: I like to cook. Roasts. Burgers. That's my speciality

B: Yum

SANDRA: I can't seem to get enough red meat. I take iron tablets

A: Are you anaemic?

SANDRA: I actually bought some from the chemist on my way here. My handbag's full of 'em!

A: I think we saw …

B: When we were looking for your phone

SANDRA: I don't take all of those at once

B: No, that's

A: We didn't look closely, we/

SANDRA: Some of those are for/

A: You don't need to explain/

B: That's completely private/

SANDRA: Anaemia's not a big deal

A: I think it's very/

SANDRA: Common. You probably have it!

B: We'll call you

A: Yes

B: Once we've seen everyone. Made our decision

SANDRA: Great

A: Are you okay getting home?

SANDRA: Absolutely

A: We'll walk you to/

SANDRA: No need!

A: It was/

SANDRA: Very nice meeting you

B: Yeah

SANDRA: Sorry. About

A: Don't/
B: Even mention it
A: Bye

A brief pause.

SANDRA: Did you ah, say I was out for about two minutes?
A: Unconscious?
B: Closer to three …
A: I'd say four minutes
SANDRA: Did I, ah, was I still, I mean/
B: 'Still'?
SANDRA: Did I shake, did I/
A: Fit?
SANDRA: 'Fit'! No, 'fit' sounds extreme I/
B: I'm not/
A: I didn't notice any shaking/
B: Possibly?/
SANDRA: It's nothing/
A: I'm not sure/
SANDRA: I knew I'd gone too hard at the gym last night. Aiming for the next City2Surf

SCENE SEVEN

SANDRA, *dressed in a witch Halloween costume, carries three large takeaway coffee cups.*

SANDRA: Spiced pumpkin lattes. Happy Halloween!
B: And you are …
SANDRA: Sandra
B: Sandra
A: Happy Halloween
SANDRA: I hope you both drink coffee

A *removes the plastic top from their paper cup and pours in some whisky.* B *does the same.*

A: 'Course

B: Cheers!
SANDRA: I saw the Halloween decorations in your house photos
B: Trick or treat?
SANDRA: I only brought the lattes I'm afraid
B: Do *you* want a trick or treat?
SANDRA: No lolly for me, I'm trying to stay off sugar
A: You may have noticed the whisky. In the lattes
SANDRA: Oh?
A: We're not
SANDRA: Sure
A: It's dad's whisky
B: It's just for Halloween
A: He left it
B: He'd want us to finish it
A: We're trying to make this as fun as possible
SANDRA: It's only once a year
B: We want to make the interviews easy on everyone
A: So we've got a couple of bottles of wine going
B: To be honest
A: We're a little drunk
SANDRA: Oh, I, couldn't tell …
B: You're our ninth interview
SANDRA: Right
A: I don't think they liked us
SANDRA: The other housemates?
A: Mum and dad
B: We don't care who moves in
SANDRA: I can move in this week
A: As long as they're fun
SANDRA: I'm looking for something long term
A: One of us is going to have to go to the bottle-O
B: Helps the medicine go down
A: The medicine being the awkward interviews
SANDRA: I hope I'm not being too awkward
A: [*sipping their boozy latte*] That's better
SANDRA: Good
B: Let's get on with it

SANDRA: It's a great house
B: It's our parents'
SANDRA: They don't, do they live/
A: They don't live here
SANDRA: Of course
B: They moved to Thailand
SANDRA: Oh
B: Last week
A: Mum says we're not hunted by wild bears anymore, there's no need for us to live in packs to survive
SANDRA: I'm sure Thailand's lovely
A: Do you like vodka?
B: I do, I have to say. Would you like a glass of something?
A: We have red and/
SANDRA: I'm okay, thank you
B: There's also the champagne the first interview brought us
SANDRA: I might finish my latte first
A: A little vodka in your latte?
SANDRA: I'm fine
B: You don't drink?
SANDRA: Dry October
A: Are you vegetarian?
SANDRA: I am
A: Someone said they were vegetarian …
B: We're not
SANDRA: I mean I'm trying to eat more greens
A: The wine's filtered through fish bladders
SANDRA: I'm coming from a pretty low base of vegetable eating
A: You did say you're a good cook
SANDRA: I try
B: We're not the cleanest people
SANDRA: I'm not obsessive, I/
A: We share the load
B: Sunday afternoon
A: Bin collection's Monday
B: So Sunday afternoon's when we do our adulting
A: Sure you don't want some of this whisky?

SANDRA: No, thank you/

A: Vodka?

B: Yes!

A: We're having a Halloween party tonight

SANDRA: Fun

B: Was that a yes to the vodka?

SANDRA: Well, I/

A: Beer?

SANDRA: None for me/

B: Cider?

SANDRA: I'm on antibiotics

A: So?

SANDRA: And they say you're not supposed to …

B: It'll make them work better!

SANDRA: I don't think so, I/

A: When they first developed antibiotics they prescribed it to almost all of the men in world war two because they were coming home with syphilis and STIs and the doctors told them that they mustn't drink while they're on this new miracle drug called antibiotics because it'll stop them from working … actually it was just a way of getting them sober so they wouldn't chase the local ladies and get infected in the first place. So drink up!

SANDRA: It's, I'm actually part of a clinical trial

A: They do that at my uni

B: Pays pretty well

SANDRA: Yeah

A: But you might grow an extra finger

B: Cheers!

A: Cheers!

They drink.

SANDRA: I think alcohol stops them working

A: Fuck 'em. The doctors won't know you've drank. You'll still get paid

B: Just one

A: Teeny tiny little drink

B: You're about our mum's age and she can drink us under the table

SANDRA: Really, I/
B: Go on
A: Don't make us feel bad!
B: We look like pissheads!
A: We need to warm up for the party
A: Shot!
B: Shot!
SANDRA: No thank you

A *and* B *drink ...*

A: Shot!
B: Shot!
A: Shot!
B: Shot!
SANDRA: I won't, thanks
A: Shot!
B: Shot!
A: Shot!
B: Shot!
A: Shot!
B: Shot!
A: That's enough
B: Whisky's finished anyway

B *exits. Music seeps in from a neighbouring Halloween party.*

A: Party animals next door
SANDRA: Loud are they?
A: Dad called the cops on them every weekend
SANDRA: I've got heavy duty earplugs
A: Some people are so irresponsible
SANDRA: The noise wouldn't bother me

B *returns, wearing some of his mother's clothes and carrying a bottle of ...*

A: Tequila!
B: We're out of lemon
A: You're sour enough
A: [*to* SANDRA] You're still here?

B: She's still here

SANDRA: I'm very interested in the room

B: Yeah?

A *pours two shots.*

SANDRA: Me too please

B: That's more like it

A *makes it three.*

A: Cheers!/

B: Cheers!

SANDRA: Cheers!

SANDRA *hesitates. She dives in and takes her first drink.*

B: She's in

A: [*to* SANDRA] Welcome to the party

B: What's the time?

A: Four thirty

B: Where is everyone?

A: Not coming until six. [*To* SANDRA] It's Mexican day of the dead themed, so passing out is encouraged

They toast.

B: To Sandra!

A: To Sandra!

SANDRA: Thanks for having me

They drink another couple of rounds. B *fires up the karaoke machine.*

B: This one's for mummy

B *starts to sing Dusty Springfield's 'You don't own me'.*

A *joins in. They pull* SANDRA *in. They sing and dance.* SANDRA*'s tentative at first, but becomes the most enthusiastic of the three. As they near the final few lines of the song* SANDRA *yells over the music ...*

SANDRA: When can I move in?

B: *What?*

SANDRA: Which day?

B: *Move in?*
SANDRA: *What day?*
B: The room's gone
A: Someone took it this afternoon

A beat. SANDRA *stops dancing.*

B: We had a lot of interviews before you
SANDRA: No, you
A: So many interviews …

A pause.

The blow is harder to take for the alcohol buzz. SANDRA *feels very dizzy.*

B: Has anyone ever told you Sandra, that you have amazing skin?
A: It looks very soft, see-through
B: I could touch your face and put my finger right through your cheek

The hat or scarf covering Sandra's hair falls off. A *and* B *run their hands over her head.*

Are you in the military?
A: It feels like a puppy!
SANDRA: Alcohol interacts with … I need to …
B: You don't have to go
A: Definitely stay for the party
SANDRA: … Bathroom

SCENE EIGHT

SANDRA *wears a public hospital-issue ill-fitting wig.*

SANDRA: Hi
A: Er …
SANDRA: Your three o'clock. I'm five minutes late
A: Oh you're here about the room?
SANDRA: Yes. Sandra
A: I thought you were coming yesterday
SANDRA: Three o'clock

A: On Saturday
SANDRA: It's five past. I've kept you waiting
A: Sunday, today's Sunday/
SANDRA: Sunday/
A: Yes/
SANDRA: Did we say Saturday?
A: We did
SANDRA: Oops
A: Sorry
SANDRA: I'm here now
A: I'm afraid the room's no longer available
SANDRA: You/
A: I'm sorry if there's been a mix up
SANDRA: My phone died
A: Someone accepted this morning
SANDRA: Lost my charger …
A: Is that a hospital tag on your wrist?
SANDRA: … I don't have a spare
A: You've come from the hospital?
SANDRA: I had a mole removed
A: Are you/
SANDRA: A freckle. Too many summers at Coogee
A: Okay?
SANDRA: Manly. The Palm Beach years …
A: You stayed overnight for that?
SANDRA: It was cosmetic, the removal, vanity, it wasn't …
A: But you were admitted, you/
SANDRA: I'm appalling with pain. After the drugs, I fell asleep, I was woozy I guess I had too many, I should have told them I'd skipped lunch. I woke up this morning and realised it was the next day. A real Medicare bender
A: I once had to stay in hospital overnight after a colonoscopy. I was getting stomach cramps, it turned out to only be my student diet! My dead-beat boyfriend at the time was supposed to pick me up after the procedure. He never showed, I was floppy on the anaesthetic, but didn't need to stay overnight, they just wanted to cover themselves, the hospital

SANDRA: Exactly

A: They're worried about you floating dreamily in front of a car so they insist on keeping you overnight even though it's nothing

SANDRA: They confirmed, this person, you're sure they're taking the room?

A: Yes

SANDRA: You don't have, do you, it was just the one

A: Only the one room

A brief pause.

Sorry

SANDRA: Do you think there's any chance …

A: You never know

SANDRA: People change their mind

A: Possibly

SANDRA: Say they're going to go to something, be somewhere and have no intention of …

A: She might

SANDRA: Nobody follows through anymore

A: It happens, if it does

SANDRA: Say things they don't mean

A: I'll give you a call

SANDRA: I'd appreciate that

A brief pause.

I've got to get back to the hospital

A: You didn't sign out?

SANDRA: I left some of my things

A: They didn't put everything together for you?

SANDRA: Junior doctor, I don't think he knew what he was doing

A: Oh

SANDRA: I was released

A: Of course

SANDRA: Discharged, not 'released'

A: [*kindly*] You weren't 'locked up'

SANDRA: It wasn't anything, no, psychiatric. I didn't want you to think I was a no-show

A: Have you been looking for a room for long?

SANDRA: Not too long

A: I've lived here for 15 years. It was my mother's house. I usually put 'women only please' in the ad and every time I get a handful of emails from men, 'fuck off and die with your cats I hope they eat you' type thing. I tell myself it's the stress of finding a place that makes people crazy. Even cave-men had caves. One guy said that in an email

SANDRA: I went to see a house on Wednesday—I guess they filled the room and forgot to cancel their interviews. I turn up at our agreed time—I got the day right with this one

A: [*kindly*] I think that helps

SANDRA: I ring the bell and hear people whispering 'shhhh'. I peer through the window and there's four people crouching under the dining room table. One woman trying to flatten herself behind the door

They laugh, they like each other.

A: Tea or a coffee?

SANDRA: I've got to go

A: These are good biscuits …

SANDRA: The hospital might pawn my possessions for a new MRI machine

A: From David Jones. I try to make a good impression. You can stay for a biscuit

SANDRA: I came straight from the hospital

A: Your current housemates will be worried

SANDRA: They'll wonder where I was last night

A: They'll think you met someone in the waiting room

SANDRA: Maybe I went home with my doctor

A: There is a bed shortage …

SANDRA: One less milligram of anaesthetic and maybe I would have woken up in time. A little extra pain

A short beat.

Did you ever get to the end of *Ulysses*? On your bookshelf

A: You read?

SANDRA: 'yes and his heart was going like mad and yes i said yes i will yes'. Then they presumably get married but you know it's not going to last

A: I've started a book club. Second Tuesday of the month. Last month was the first. You should come. You should join

SANDRA: I don't get a lot of time to/

A: There's only three of us so far. We meet here in my living room. Seven o'clock. It's not serious. This month's book is *Emma*. Last month was *American Psycho*. We're very broad

SANDRA: … Read as much as I'd like

A: Amanda—the woman who's taking the room? Said she's not much of a reader which probably means this month will just be the three of us again—two if Sam is in Newcastle for work—you should come. It'll be fun

SANDRA: Okay

A: Yeah?

SANDRA: That'd be nice

A: I take care of the wine and nibbles. You can bring a plate if you like. You've a little over three weeks to read the book

SANDRA: I'll finish it

A: I'm glad you came

SANDRA: Me too

A: I was really looking for a housemate so you know, this isn't just a recruitment drive for my under-attended book club

SANDRA: I'll read it this weekend

A: You'll like the others, they're a laugh

SANDRA: I look forward to it

A: Last month we barely even talked about the book to be honest

SANDRA: Has this other person paid a deposit yet for the room?

A: Amanda? Not yet

SANDRA: She hasn't put down any money?

A: Would you like to borrow my copy of *Emma*? Save you buying one?

SANDRA: So you could cancel, you could say …

A: That I changed my mind? I'd like to, but I can't do that!

SANDRA: People say things they don't mean

A: Not me, I/

SANDRA: Say yes to things they have no intention of doing

A: Sandra

SANDRA: It's only been a few hours, it's not as if you're reneging on the day she's due to move in. Send her another text

A: If she cancels, I'll call you

SANDRA: Say you messaged the wrong person this morning. Tell her you meant to offer the room to someone else, you confused our phone numbers

A: If I had done that, I'd still have to honour it

SANDRA: You noticed your mistake, you're humiliated

A: I would be

SANDRA: Send her another text

A: I do some volunteer work for the Cancer Council. They have a community program, all you need to do is register with the website, let them know when your next appointment is with your nurse or your radiation oncologist and a volunteer will pick you up from your home, drive you to the appointment, sit in the waiting room, or go in with you if you like, and take you home again. They're not counsellors but they're trained, you can talk to them. They'll get you a naturalistic wig, they can even match your usual hairstyle. I have a pamphlet

SANDRA *puts her hand into the biscuit tin and takes two biscuits.* SANDRA *stuffs her biscuits into* A*'s mouth.* A *chokes.*

What are you doing?!

SANDRA *shoves more biscuits in. She is consumed with rage.* A *fights her off,* SANDRA *is too weak to fight back, she falls back exhausted and* A *recovers.*

A: Get out! I'll call the police!

SCENE NINE

SANDRA *holds a bag in each hand.*

B: Jackie moved her stuff out this morning. She scrubbed it after, I saw her, so I can tell ya it's all clean

SANDRA *grips her bags.*

We thought this room might be best for ya because it's next to the toilet. Some of the rooms don't have a toilet on the same floor and it's a good couple a minutes walk. Your referral said you have a medical thing. Don't worry, I don't know what it is, it's private, we put everyone who has a health condition near a toilet even if it turns out they have like, a mental problem or something which has nothing to do with needing the loo. Otherwise it's grab whatever bed's free, everything's mixed up here.

SANDRA *looks around the room.*

Most of the geezers in here are ex-drinkers, used to drinking nothing but alcohol for thirty years. Now they're off the booze, they hardly drink anything at all, need the toilet only once a day and it's dark, you can imagine when it finally comes out, sometimes they forget to flush and I don't need to imagine, I see it, it's dark orange or brown, very unhealthy, so they can walk, that's what I'm saying, a walk up the stairs once a day does them good.

Anyway they'll get liver stones, the lot of them

SANDRA: Kidney

B: What's that for?

SANDRA: You mean kidney stones

B: I don't snore or nuthin. I don't mind if you do

SANDRA: I don't snore

B: Wanna know how everything works?

SANDRA: Go on

B: Breakfast is between six and eight, lunch is up to you and dinner is five to seven. Kitchen's on the third floor, we'll go there next. We have a barbecue every now and again on the roof. Sausages and that. There's a roster. Do you like cooking?

SANDRA: No

B: Everyone does something. You can cook, do the gardening, clean, settle people in like I do. Whatever you like. You need anything, want to ask a question, ask me. I've been here three years

SANDRA: I only need something short term

B: I thought I'd be outta here in a few months. Barry on the fourth floor said he'd only need the bed a week, we had his fifth year anniversary last month

SANDRA: I won't be here long

B: For all I know you got a flush Nigerian Prince sending you money and you're just waiting for it to clear

A brief pause.

At night we watch TV in the rec room, play cards, go out if you like, it's a hostel not a prison. You, ah, put a lot of your stuff in that drawer. The third drawer's the one we share. Well it's my drawer, but I'll let you put some things in it. You're going to have to take out your towel, those socks. They're bulky. Your toothbrush being in there is probably okay

No response from SANDRA.

Take out your towel
Get rid of those socks
I don't want your toothbrush there
This is my room. I'm happy to share it
Take them out

No response from SANDRA.

Take them out

No response from SANDRA.

Take them out

No response from SANDRA.

Take them out

No response from SANDRA.

Take them out

No response from SANDRA.

Take them out

No response from SANDRA.

Take them out

No response from SANDRA.

Take them out

No response from SANDRA.

Keep to your side

B *walks towards* SANDRA.*He puts his hand into one of her bags and pokes around.* SANDRA *urinates onto the rug.*

SANDRA: This half of the room is my territory

B: Dogs like having their own space to sleep, and a separate space to piss and shit. Guess you're okay doing everything in here?

SANDRA *does the best she can to arrange her bed.*

Go off to die, did you know that? They leave their pack, dogs do, when it's time, they don't wanna know ya

SANDRA *lays down.*

I'm going downstairs to watch the footy

SANDRA *tries to sleep.*

I hope you weren't expecting to tune our TV to *Cupcake Wars*

No reaction from SANDRA.

Or flippin *Sex and the City*, I'm telling ya, you won't get a look in

No reaction from SANDRA.

I used to play footy
I was a forward, you wouldn't know what that is
That means I/

SANDRA: I'm trying to sleep

B: Played properly in my day, if ya didn't have a bloody nose five minutes in, you weren't really tryin

SANDRA: I need to rest

B: Played a full match with a fractured wrist once. I reckon a concussion

SANDRA: I'm very tired

B: No doctors on the sideline, did we. Dislocated my shoulder, I still didn't go off, just smacked it back into place against the goal post and kept goin

SANDRA: Will you shut/

B: Straight into the scrum. I had to

SANDRA: Shut up!

B: Not for me

SANDRA: Shut up!

B: Had the team to think of

SANDRA: Ha! 'The team'

B: They were countin' on me

SANDRA: Where's your team now?

B: Achilles

SANDRA: They dumped you

B: No I can't play anymore

SANDRA: You relied on them. You couldn't look after yourself. Look at you. You still can't. You've always been hoping and begging to be picked by a side, haven't you, it's up to everybody else whether you get a run onto the field

B: I was the roughest forward those guys ever/

SANDRA: That's why you're here. This is where you've always been heading. Because you walk around out there with your dirt smudged and your greasy sweat showing, you've got to look at tennis if you want to understand how this works

B: I play fair. I never cheated

SANDRA: Tennis is the scrappiest, most brutal game there is but it pretends to be all white elegance, calm and dignified. With tennis there's no clubs or team colours or social part to the game. There's nothing to belong to. Golfers have caddies to whisper to, boxers think they're so tough, but they all have someone in their corner, tennis players are out there all alone and they know it. Nobody plays harder than them

B: No team mates, who are they playing for?

SANDRA: They fight for themselves. They don't need anyone else, not even someone to compete with. Find a back fence or a graffitied brick wall and you can play for yourself, hit the ball back and forth. Three years. Look at you. A mess. You're not even trying. I only need something short term

SANDRA *preens, tries to fix herself up.*

B: This ain't an orphanage. No rich godmother's gunna come through here and rescue the prettiest looking kid

SANDRA: I don't know why I even unpacked. I *will* take out my socks. My towel is going back in my bag thank-you-very-much. I don't require any space. I won't be here soon. Only for tonight

B: Tomorrow night's been paid for, you should at least/

SANDRA: You're not my coach. I won't take advice from you. Fighting over drawer space! All white elegance, calm and dignified. Nobody fights harder than me. Sitting around waiting for your team. Three years! I don’t need anyone else. Tomorrow. I’ll be. I don’t even need my toothbrush out. I’m packed. All white elegance. I’ll find a back fence or a graffitied brick wall and I’ll keep hitting the ball back and forth, for yourself, it’s only ever been you but that’s ok, that’s how it is forever until

END OF PLAY

GRIFFIN THEATRE COMPANY
PRESENTS

GOOD COOK. FRIENDLY. CLEAN.

BROOKE ROBINSON

4 MAY – 16 JUNE

Director Marion Potts
Designer Melanie Liertz
Lighting Designer Alexander Berlage
Sound Designer & Composer Nate Edmondson
Stage Manager Khym Scott
With Fayssal Bazzi, Tara Morice, Kelly Paterniti

SBW Stables Theatre
Preview 4 – 8 May
Season 11 May – 16 June

Government Partners

Griffin acknowledges the generosity of the Seaborn, Broughton & Walford Foundation in allowing it the use of the SBW Stables Theatre rent free, less outgoings, since 1986.

Supported by

PLAYWRIGHT'S NOTE

In 2015, I moved to London, and after 10 years of renting my own unit in Sydney, I was back on the shared accommodation market. If you're in Paris, London, San Francisco or Sydney, renting a room in shared accommodation usually means pitching yourself to a panel of twenty-to-thirty something housemates and hoping that from the dozens (or hundreds) of applicants they've received, they decide to pick you. Just as most people who apply for any individual job vacancy won't be invited to interview, it's not easy to even get a chance to see the room and meet your would-be housemates, let alone impress them. There is a great deal of luck and stress involved and you never really know what any particular household is looking for in their new housemate. A friend in London offered his spare room to an applicant who said they had a waffle maker—that turned out to be the deciding factor for him. I was offered my current room in North London because my housemates were impressed with my turning up to the interview in shoes without socks. They thought this made me seem laidback. And there is one thing everybody wants in a housemate: you must be laidback. It is imperative to be relaxed and chilled and cool at a housemate interview. You may have been evicted yesterday, you may be sleeping on a friend's couch without a dollar to your name, you might be waiting for the dole to hit your bank account, but you must appear to be laidback. If you're tired, if you're sick of talking about yourself because it's the third housemate interview you've had that day, you simply won't sell yourself well and you will not be offered a room. I mention the waffle maker because if you're on one side of this situation, it might be flippant and funny, but if you're on the other side, it might mean you'll be sleeping in a tent in Martin Place.

There aren't many 'spare room' ads that say they're willing to take a housemate in their forties. The ground really thins out if you're in your fifties. If you're approaching or past sixty, and you can't afford to buy or rent a property for yourself, and you don't quite qualify for a state government housing place (or you're waiting on the agonisingly long list), then I have no idea what you're supposed to do. I do know that you would have very little control of your living situation, that you would likely have to sleep under any mouldy/noisy/uncomfortable/unsafe roof that would take you, and that's if you had a roof at all.

For a short time in the UK, I had a housemate well into her fifties who ran miles around North London every day. She was desperate to keep fit because the moment her health went, her whole minimum-wage-casual-job-paying-rent-week-by-week house of cards situation would come tumbling down very, very quickly. The future is incredibly frightening.

Brooke Robinson
Writer

DIRECTOR'S NOTE

At this point in time, we are two weeks away from starting rehearsals. We are almost two months away from opening night. There is so much we don't know about this play, and so many discoveries ahead.

This is what we do know:

- Brooke Robinson has written a play that has had a magic effect on actors. There's a performativity in the writing that speaks directly to theatre artists, inviting them to flex their imaginative muscles. It throws down a gauntlet to designers and a director. So many plays fail to invite such theatricality, but this one calls out to dance with an audience.
- The play is funny until it's really not. There's a stylistic sophistication in the writing that makes us dread what we enjoy and enjoy what we are dreading. The way the play asks the most extreme parts of our selves to co-exist in a single shared room creates an intense vacuum of critical observation. Within one hour of stage time, or one scene or even one moment, there is humour and heartache, compassion and brutality, self-knowledge and delusion.
- The play begs a strong question that goes well beyond ageism, or the housing crisis, or the shallow state of Sydney's culture. The play interrogates the nature of community and sets us a series of questions to answer—about who we are, what we value, and how we aspire to live.
- The play isn't really about Sydney. Sydney is a heightened setting here and a clever one because it smacks with familiarity and locates us within it, reminding us that we're seeing elements in real time. But it's a blindingly bright, over-saturated, MSG-enhanced Sydney—a city at its worst when we are at our worst. The setting is potentially anywhere where there's a promise of community and safety that can just as easily protect you as it can kick the trust out of you. It's the logical extension of rampant individualism, a city that lies at the end of our own selfish road.
- The play suggests that it's about generational difference, but it seems to be about maturity, responsibility and accountability. Sandra is the only character who has an age, who has earned her right to a name, and whose lived experience has given her an identity. It seems to be about what happens when power is held in the hands of childish adults, people who almost infantilise themselves, just so they can continue living with the sweetness of lollipops.
- Once communities erode, we're left with tenuous bonds. We're only really connected by the electricity grid, by waste disposal services, by sewerage pipes, and by the residual history of the hearths and the houses that we pass through.

These are some of the ideas that have kick-started our production, and which we look forward to exploring further.

Marion Potts
Director

Brooke Robinson

Playwright

Brooke is a playwright from Sydney, currently based in London. Her credits as a playwright include: for Red Line Productions: *The Telescope;* for Tamarama Rock Surfers: *Animal/People;* for Old 505 Theatre and The Sub Station: *Dangerous Lenses.* Brooke is a graduate of ATYP's Fresh Ink writers ensemble, Stephen Jeffreys' invitational writers group at the Royal Academy of Dramatic Art (London), and is a current member of The Criterion Theatre's invitational West End writers group, led by Greg Mosse. She was one of six artists to be commissioned for *Imagine 2037*, the imaginary theatre festival for the British Council's 20th Anniversary Edinburgh Festival Showcase, and was shortlisted for Matthew Warchus' inaugural *Old Vic 12* playwriting commission at the Old Vic Theatre in London. *Good Cook. Friendly. Clean.* was shortlisted for the 2017 Griffin Award and was read at London's Bunker Theatre as part of the Damsel Women Directors' Festival.

Marion Potts

Director

Marion has worked with many of the country's leading theatre companies and has held senior positions with Bell Shakespeare (Associate Artistic Director), Malthouse Theatre (Artistic Director/CEO) and Sydney Theatre Company (Resident Director). In this time she has directed over 50 productions including for Griffin: *Ugly Mugs, The Story of the Miracles at Cookie's Table, Wonderlands*; for Bell Shakespeare: *Hamlet, King Lear, Othello, The Taming of the Shrew*; for Malthouse Theatre: *Blood Wedding, The Dragon, Hate, Meow Meow's Little Match Girl* (including its return season at the Southbank Centre in London), *Sappho... in 9 fragments, 'Tis Pity She's a Whore, The Riders* (with Victorian Opera and Western Australian Opera), *Ugly Mugs, Venus & Adonis* (with Bell Shakespeare), *Wild Surmise;* for Melbourne Theatre Company: *Di and Viv and Rose, Grace;* for STCSA: *A Number, Equus, Gary's House, The Goat or Who Is Sylvia?, The Torrents*; for Sydney Theatre Company*: The Blessing, The Café Latte Kid, Closer, The Crucible, Cyrano de Bergerac, Del Del, Don Juan, The Herbal Bed, Life After George, Navigating, Playgrounds, Pygmalion, Two Weeks With The Queen, Volpone, What is the Matter With Mary Jane?, Where Are We Now?,* and *The Wonderful World of Dissocia*; for Queensland Theatre: *Constance Drinkwater and the Final Days of Somerset*. Marion has received numerous awards including a Helpmann Award for Best Direction of a Play for *The Goat or Who Is Sylvia?* Marion is currently Executive Producer with Performing Lines.

Melanie Liertz

Designer

Melanie is a freelance designer and maker for theatre, film, dance and circus. Her theatre design credits include: for ATYP: *Oedipus Doesn't Live Here Anymore;* for La Mama: *Yarn and Button;* for Malthouse Theatre: *This is Beautiful*; for Melbourne Theatre Company: *Yellow Moon*; for NICA: *Dreams from the Second Floor;* for Q Theatre: *Frankenstein;* for Sport for Jove: *Antigone,* for which Melanie won two Sydney Theatre Awards for Set Design for an Independent Theatre Production and Costume Design for an Independent Theatre Production, *No End of Blame;* for Sydney Festival: *Alice in Wonderland;* for Sydney Opera House: *Funatorium: Captain Hook's Pirate Party.* Her costume design credits include: for Pinchgut Opera: *Triple Bill*; for Sport for Jove: *Edward II, Love's Labour's Lost* (Sydney Theatre Award nomination). Melanie has also worked as a costume maker for companies including Australian Ballet, Bell Shakespeare, BighART, Legs on the Wall, Malthouse Theatre, Sydney Chamber Opera, and Victorian Opera. Melanie graduated from the Victorian College of the Arts with a Bachelor of Creative Arts.

Alexander Berlage

Lighting Designer

Alexander Berlage is a Sydney-based lighting designer and director. His lighting design credits include: for Griffin Independent: *Nosferatutu or Bleeding at the Ballet, Thomas Murray and the Upside Down River*; for ATYP: *Between Us, Luke Lloyd: Alienoid, Moth, War Crimes*; for Critical Stages: *4000 Miles, Songs for the Fallen, Stones in his Pockets*; for Ensemble Theatre: *Buyer and Cellar, The Kitchen Sink*; for Hayes Theatre: *Dogfight, Everybody Loves Lucy, High Fidelity*; for Old 505 Theatre: *The Block Universe, Hilt, Home Invasion*; for Red Line Productions and Workhorse Theatre Company: *4:48 Psychosis,* for which he won the 2017 Sydney Theatre Award for Best Lighting Designer for an Independent Production, *Crimes of the Heart, Doubt* (Sydney Theatre Award nomination), *Freak Winds, Howie the Rookie, Men, there will be a climax, The Bitter Tears of Petra Von Kant* (Sydney Theatre Award nomination), *The Judas Kiss, The Whale* (Sydney Theatre Award nomination); for Sydney Chamber Opera: *Victory Over the Sun*; for Sydney Dance Company: *PPY15: Revealed*; for Sydney Theatre Company: *Cloud Nine, Lethal Indifference*. His director credits include: for An Assorted Few: *The Van De Maar Papers*; for Old 505 Theatre and An Assorted Few: *Home Invasion*; for Red Line Productions and An Assorted Few: *there will be a climax.*

Nate Edmondson

Sound Designer & Composer

Nate is an international, multi-award winning composer and sound designer for stage and screen. His theatre credits include: for Griffin: *Caress/Ache, Jump for Jordan, This Year's Ashes, The Witches*; for Griffin Independent: *The Ham Funeral, Rust and Bone, MinusOneSister, Music*; for ATYP: *Fireface, The Hiding Place, Political Children*; for Bell Shakespeare: *A Midsummer Night's Dream, Macbeth, Romeo and Juliet, The Tempest, The Winter's Tale*; for Belvoir: *Mark Colvin's Kidney, Mortido, Seventeen, This Heaven*; for Darlinghurst Theatre Company: *All My Sons, Daylight Saving, Good Works, Savages, The Seafarer, The Paris Letter, Torch Song Trilogy*; for Ensemble Theatre: *Diplomacy*; for KXT/bAKEHOUSE: *Jatinga, Leaves, Straight*; for Little Ones Theatre: *Psycho Beach Party, Salomé, Two by Two*; for New Theatre: *Marat/Sade, When The Rain Stops Falling*; for Red Line Productions: *Bengal Tiger at the Baghdad Zoo, I Am My Own Wife, The Village Bike*; for Rockefeller Productions: *That Golden Girls Show!* (US), *The Very Hungry Caterpillar Show* (AU, NZ, US, UAE & UK); for Seymour Centre: *Blackrock, The Flick*; for Siren Theatre Company: *Good With Maps* (AU & UK), *Misterman* (AU & UK), *The Trouble With Harry* (AU & UK); for Sport For Jove: *Of Mice and Men*; for Street Theatre: *All My Sons* (UK); for Sydney Dance Company: *Once We Were*; for Sydney Theatre Company: *A Midsummer Night's Dream, Cloud Nine, Never Did Me Any Harm* (with Force Majeure), *Romeo and Juliet, Three Sisters*.

Khym Scott

Stage Manager

Khym was the stage manager for Griffin's *Kill Climate Deniers, Festival of New Writing, Girl in Tan Boots, The Serpent's Table,* and *The Witches.* From 2013 to 2017 he was assistant stage manager of The Australian Ballet, and toured regionally (as stage manager), nationally, and internationally. Other recent credits include: for Belvoir: *This Heaven, Miss Julie;* for Performance 4a: *Stories Then and Now;* for Sydney Festival: *Lady Rizo: Red, White and Indigo.* He has also stage managed for Sydney Gay and Lesbian Mardi Gras. Khym is a graduate of NIDA and The University of Sydney.

Fayssal Bazzi

Character B

Fayssal's theatre credits include for Griffin Theatre Company: *Lord of the Flies, The Pigeons;* for Belvoir: *Sami in Paradise, Back at the Dojo, Ivanov, The Government Inspector, Food*; for Bell Shakespeare: *The Merchant of Venice*; for B Sharp/Arts Radar: *Woyzeck*; for Black Swan State Theatre Company: *The Motherf**cker with the Hat*; for Darlinghurst Theatre Company: *I Only Came to Use the Phone*; for Malthouse Theatre: *Timeshare;* for New Theatre: *Don Juan in Soho*; for Red Line Productions: *Poster Girl, Sprout, Redemption, This Blasted Earth: A Christmas Miracle with Music*; for Riverside Theatres Parramatta: *All the Blood and All the Water*; for Seymour Centre: *Love, Madness and Poetry; To the Green Fields Beyond*; for Sydney Opera House: *Cross Sections*; for Sydney Theatre Company: *Look the Other Way*. Fayssal's film credits include: *6 Days, Cedar Boys, Down Under, Emulsion, The Merger*, and playing the voice of 'Mr Todd' in *Peter Rabbit*. His television credits include *All Saints, Chosen, Crownies, Double the Fist, East West 101, The Strip, Stupid Stupid Man, Top of the Lake: China Girl* and *Wake in Fright.*

Tara Morice

Sandra

A graduate of the National Institute of Dramatic Art, Tara has worked extensively in theatre, film and television. Her first film out of NIDA was Baz Luhrmann's *Strictly Ballroom,* for which she was nominated for a British Academy of Film and Television Award (BAFTA), an Australian Film Institute Award (AFI) and a Film Critics Circle award. Her other films include *Candy, Hotel Sorrento, Hildegarde, Metalskin, Moulin Rouge, Oranges and Sunshine, Razzle Dazzle* and the Oscar-nominated short *Miracle Fish.* Tara was most recently seen in the feature *Dance Academy: The Movie* and will next be seen in the independent feature *Reaching Distance*. Tara's television credits include *Answered By Fire, After The Deluge, A Difficult Woman,* the Logie-winning and Emmy-nominated series *Dance Academy, Dogwoman, Grass Roots, Loot, McLeod's Daughters, My Husband My Killer, Playschool, Salem's Lot, Water Rats*, and *Winter.* On stage, Tara has performed with Griffin in *After Dinner, The Moonwalkers,* and *Wolf Lullaby* as well as in productions for Bell Shakespeare, Belvoir, Ensemble Theatre, Malthouse Theatre, Queensland Theatre and Sydney Theatre Company, and has been nominated for a Green Room Award and a Helpmann Award for her work in musical theatre productions. Tara wrote, produced and directed the documentary *My Biggest Fan*, which premiered at the Fort Lauderdale International Film Festival and screened on SBS. As a singer, Tara recorded *Time After Time* for the *Strictly Ballroom* soundtrack, and a new version for the album *Something For Everybody*. She has also narrated documentaries for the ABC, SBS and National Geographic.

Kelly Paterniti

Character A

Kelly's theatre credits include: for Griffin Theatre Company: *Emerald City*; for Griffin Independent and mt productions; *Dealing With Clair*; for Griffin Independent and Two Birds One Stone: *S-27*; for Bell Shakespeare: *As You Like It, Romeo and Juliet*; for the Blue Room Studio: *Dirty Pretty Nails;* for Essential Theatre: *Romeo and Juliet*; for Hayman Theatre Company: *A Midsummer Night's Dream, The Shawl, The Trojan Women*; for Sydney Theatre Company: *A Flea in Her Ear*; for WA Youth Theatre Company: *Cloudstreet*. Her film credits include: *Griff the Invisible, Redd Inc.,* and *Skinford.* For television, Kelly has performed in: *Australia: The Story of Us, Home and Away, Cops LAC, Packed to the Rafters, Stormworld* and *Wormwood.* Kelly attended John Curtin College of the Arts and furthered her studies at Curtin University.

ABOUT GRIFFIN

GRIFFIN THEATRE COMPANY
13 CRAIGEND ST
KINGS CROSS NSW 2011

02 9332 1052
INFO@GRIFFINTHEATRE.COM.AU
GRIFFINTHEATRE.COM.AU

SBW STABLES THEATRE
10 NIMROD ST
KINGS CROSS NSW 2011

BOOKINGS
GRIFFINTHEATRE.COM.AU
02 9361 3817

"If you've ever sat in the theatre and thought, 'those actors are just too damn far away', then Griffin is for you." – Concrete Playground

Located in the heart of Kings Cross—in the historic SBW Stables Theatre—Griffin has been dedicated to bringing the best Australian stories to the stage for the better part of four decades.

We're passionate about theatre that's written by Australians, about Australians, for Australians to enjoy. Iconic Aussie plays such as *The Boys, Holding the Man, The Heartbreak Kid* and *The Bleeding Tree* all had their world premieres at Griffin. And many of our nation's most celebrated artists started their professional careers with us – Cate Blanchett, David Wenham, Michael Gow and Louis Nowra to name a few.

Homegrown inspiration. By you, for you.

GRIFFIN FAMILY

Patron
Seaborn, Broughton & Walford Foundation

Griffin acknowledges the generosity of the Seaborn, Broughton & Walford Foundation in allowing it the use of the SBW Stables Theatre rent free, less outgoings, since 1986.

Board
Bruce Meagher (Chair), Simon Burke, Tim Duggan, Lee Lewis, Kate Mulvany, Mario Philippou, Sue Procter, Lenore Robertson, Simone Whettonn

Artistic Director & CEO
Lee Lewis

Artistic Associate
Phil Spencer

General Manager
Karen Rodgers

Associate Producer - Development
Will Harvey

Associate Producer - Marketing
Estelle Conley

Associate Producer
Nicole La Bianca

Publicist
Dino Dimitriadis

Marketing & Development Coordinator
Lucy McNabb

Communications Coordinator
Ang Collins

Program & Administration Coordinator
Madeline Parker

Strategic Insights Consultant
Peter O'Connell

Production Manager
Kirby Brierty

Production Coordinator
Dana Spence

Financial Consultant
Tracey Whitby

Finance Manager
Kylie Richards

Customer Relations Manager
Elliott Wilshier

Customer Relations Team
Maria Dimopulos, Ell Katte, Julian Larnach, Stephen Moore, Grace Nye-Butler

Brand and Graphic Design
Re

Cover Photography
Brett Boardman

GRIFFIN DONORS

Income from Griffin activities covers less than 40% of our operating costs – leaving an ever increasing gap for us to fill through government funding, sponsorship and the generosity of our individual supporters. Your support helps us bridge the gap and keep ticket prices affordable and our work at its best. To make a donation and a difference, contact Griffin on 9332 1052 or donate online at griffintheatre.com.au

Studio Program
Gil Appleton
Darin Cooper Foundation
Limb Family Foundation
Peter Graves
Ken & Lilian Horler
Rhonda McIver
Pip Rath & Wayne Lonergan
Geoff & Wendy Simpson
Danielle Smith
Walking up the Hill Foundation

A single exceptional production is chosen each year to be supported through our Production Partnerships Program

2018 PRODUCTION DONORS: KILL CLIMATE DENIERS

Production Patrons
Andrew Bell & Joanna Bird
Robert Dick & Erin Shiel
Richard McHugh & Kate Morgan
Bruce Meagher & Greg Waters

Production Partners
Anonymous
Tea Uglow
Penelope Wass

SEASON DONORS

Main Stage Donor
$5,000-$10,000
Bernard Coles
Darin Cooper Foundation
Lyndell & Daniel Droga
Peter Graves
Helen & Abraham James
Lee Lewis & Brett Boardman
Anthony & Suzanne Maple-Brown
Sophie McCarthy & Antony Green
Don & Leslie Parsonage
Sue Procter
The Robertson Foundation
The Sky Foundation
Merilyn Sleigh & Raoul de Ferranti

Final Draft
$2,000-$4,999
Gae Anderson
Ellen Borda
Alan Colletti
Richard Cottrell
Bryony & Tim Cox
Libby Higgin
Michael Hobbs
Kiong Lee & Richard Funston
David Nguyen
Peter & Dianne O'Connell
Pip Rath & Wayne Lonergan
Anthony Paull
Chris Reed
Tea Uglow
Carole & David Yuile

Workshop Donor
$1,000-$1,999
Anonymous (3)
Antoinette Albert
Helen Bauer & Helen Lynch AM
Amanda Bishop
Corinne Campbell & Bryan Everts
Peter Chapman
Elaine Chia & Ettore Altomare
Louise Christie
Terence Clarke
Sally Crawford
Cris Croker & David West
Nathan Croft & James White
Michael Diamond
Tim Duggan
Ros & Paul Epsie
John & Libby Fairfax
Judge Joe Harman
James Hartwright & Kerrin D'Arcy
Stephen Hawkins
Mary Holt
Peter Ingle
Margaret Johnston
Jennifer Ledgar & Bob Lim
Richard & Elizabeth Longes
Carina G. Martin
John McCallum
Elaine & Bill McLaughlin
Dr Wendy Michaels
Tommy Murphy
Ian Phipps
Martin Portus
Steve & Belinda Rankine
Sylvia Rosenblum
Will Sheehan
Robyn Stone
Augusta Supple
Stuart Thomas
Elizabeth Thompson
Mike Thompson
David West
Paul & Jennifer Winch
Simone Whetton
Adrian Wiggins & Siobhan Toohill
Penny Young & Ian Neuss
Elizabeth Wing

Reading Donor
$500-$999
Anonymous (1)
Jes Andersen
Wendy Ashton
Robyn Ayres
Melissa Ball
Nikki Barrett
Karen Bedford
Penny Beran
Tanja Boric
Jo Bradley
Alex Byrne & Sue Hearn
Bill Calcraft
Carol Dettmann
Louise Diamond
Max Dingle
Wendy Elder
Bob Ernst
Brian Everingham
Robyn Fortescue &

Rosie Wagstaff
Jennifer Giles
Nicky Gluyas
Erica Gray
Reg Graycar
Tonkin Zulaikha Greer
Anthony Gregg
Jennifer Hagan
Stephanie &
Andrew Harrison
John Head
Karen Henoch-Ryugo
Susan Hyde
David & Adrienne Kitching
Ian & Elizabeth MacDonald
Christopher McCabe
Nicole Mckenna
Patrick McIntyre
Dr Steve McNamara
Neville Mitchell
Catriona Morgan-Hunn
Patricia Novikoff
Alex Oonagh Redmond
Roslyn Renwick
Karen Rodgers &
Bill Harris
Gemma Rygate
Julianne Schultz
Diana Simmonds
Jann Skinner
Rob & Rae Spence
Ross Steele AM
Mary Stollery & Eric Dole
Adam Suckling
Catherine Sullivan &
Alexandra Bowen
Sue Thomson
Ariadne Vromen

First Draft Donor
$200 - $499
Anonymous (11)
Priscilla Adey
Michael Allen
Philip Batchelor
Pamela Bennett
Edwina Birch
Shay Bristowe
Wendy Buswell
Ruth Campbell
Charlie Chan &
Angela Catterns
Sue Clark
Kate Collier
Neale Craker
Bryan Cutler
Marie Delaney
Susan Donnelly
Sarah Dunn
Elizabeth Evatt
Matt Garrett
Sarah & Braith Gilchrist
Brenda Gottsche
Elizabeth Hanley
Rodney Hanratty & John Lam
Po Tang
Marie-Louise Harvey
Belinda Hazelton
Janet Heffernan
Danielle Hoareau
Mark Hopkinson &
Michelle Opie
Trish Howes
Marian & Nabeel Ibrahim
Diana Jefferson
Susan Kath
C John Keightley
Rob Koczkar & Heather Doig
Ryan Kucharski
Penelope Latey
Gary Lawrence
Peta Leemen
Antoinette Le Marchant
Dr Peter Louw
Carolyn Lowry
Anni Macdougall
Stephen Manning
Michael Markiewicz
Robert Marks
Suz Mawer
Philip McAlistair &
Fiona O'Leary
Duncan McKay
Ian Mcmillan
Kate Mulvany
Margaret Murphy
Dian Neligan
Carolyn Newman
Annie Page &
Colin Fletcher
Jane Peden
Christopher Powell
Virginia Pursell
Ann Rocca
Peter & Barbara Rooke
Catherine Rothery
Anne Schofield
Julia Selby
Michael Sirmai &
Rebecca Finkelstein
Geoffrey Starr
Stephen Thompson
Trisha Treanor
Christophe Vivien
David Walsh
Cathy Wilcox
Victoria Wildie
Aviva Ziegler

We would also like to thank Peter O'Connell for his expertise, guidance and time.

Current as of
3 March, 2018

GRIFFIN SPONSORS

Griffin would like to thank the following:

Government Supporters

Patron

2018 Season Sponsor

Production Partner

GIRGENSOHN FOUNDATION

Production Sponsor

nabprivate

Griffin Award

Griffin Studio & New Writing

Griffin Ambassadors & Artistic Assoc. Sponsor

Company Lawyers

Associate Sponsor

Company Sponsors

THE SATURDAY PAPER

Access Partners

DESIGNKINGCOMPANY

Griffin Theatre Company is assisted by the Australian Government through the Australia Council, it's arts funding and advisory body; and the NSW Government through Create NSW.